EASY BRUSS[ ]

SPROUTS

COOKBOOK

50 DELICIOUS BRUSSELS SPROUTS RECIPES

By
BookSumo Press
Copyright © by Saxonberg Associates

Published by
BookSumo Press, a DBA of Saxonberg Associates
http://www.booksumo.com/

ABOUT THE AUTHOR.

BookSumo Press is a publisher of unique, easy, and healthy cookbooks.

Our cookbooks span all topics and all subjects. If you want a deep dive into the possibilities of cooking with any type of ingredient. Then BookSumo Press is your go to place for robust yet simple and delicious cookbooks and recipes. Whether you are looking for great tasting pressure cooker recipes or authentic ethic and cultural food. BookSumo Press has a delicious and easy cookbook for you.

With simple ingredients, and even simpler step-by-step instructions BookSumo cookbooks get everyone in the kitchen chefing delicious meals.

BookSumo is an independent publisher of books operating in the beautiful Garden State (NJ) and our team of chefs and kitchen experts are here to teach, eat, and be merry!

INTRODUCTION

Welcome to *The Effortless Chef Series*! Thank you for taking the time to purchase this cookbook.

Come take a journey into the delights of easy cooking. The point of this cookbook and all BookSumo Press cookbooks is to exemplify the effortless nature of cooking simply.

In this book we focus on Brussels Sprouts. You will find that even though the recipes are simple, the taste of the dishes are quite amazing.

So will you take an adventure in simple cooking? If the answer is yes please consult the table of contents to find the dishes you are most interested in.

Once you are ready, jump right in and start cooking.

— BookSumo Press

TABLE OF CONTENTS

ANY ISSUES? CONTACT US

If you find that something important to you is missing from this book please contact us at info@booksumo.com.

We will take your concerns into consideration when the 2nd edition of this book is published. And we will keep you updated!

— BookSumo Press

LEGAL NOTES

COMMON ABBREVIATIONS

cup(s)	C.
tablespoon	tbsp
teaspoon	tsp
ounce	oz.
pound	lb

*All units used are standard American measurements

Chapter 1: Easy Brussels Sprouts Recipes

How to Bake Brussels Sprouts

Ingredients

- 1 1/2 lb. Brussels sprouts, ends trimmed and yellow leaves removed
- 3 tbsp olive oil
- 1 tsp kosher salt
- 1/2 tsp freshly ground black pepper

Directions

- Set your oven to 400 degrees F before doing anything else and arrange the rack in the center of the oven.
- In a large resealable plastic bag, add the trimmed Brussels sprouts, olive oil, kosher salt and pepper and shake to coat.
- Transfer the vegetable mixture onto a baking sheet.
- Cook in the oven for about 30-45 minutes, shaking the pan after every 5-7 minutes.
- Serve immediately.

Amount per serving (6 total)

Timing Information:

Preparation	15 m
Cooking	45 m
Total Time	1 h

Nutritional Information:

Calories	104 kcal
Fat	7.3 g
Carbohydrates	10g
Protein	2.9 g
Cholesterol	0 mg
Sodium	344 mg

* Percent Daily Values are based on a 2,000 calorie diet.

Pre-Colonial Brussels Sprouts

Ingredients

- 1 tbsp butter
- 2 cloves garlic, chopped
- 1 tbsp butter
- 6 Brussels sprouts, trimmed and halved
- 1 tbsp butter
- 2 tbsp shredded Parmesan cheese
- salt and ground black pepper to taste

Directions

- In a frying pan, melt 1 tbsp of the butter on medium heat and sauté the garlic for about 30 seconds.
- Add 1 tbsp of the butter and Brussels sprouts, cut-side down and cook, covered for about 4-6 minutes.
- Flip the Brussels sprouts and add 1 tbsp butter and cook, covered for about 3 minutes.
- Transfer the Brussels sprouts into a serving plate.
- Serve with a sprinkling of the Parmesan cheese, salt and black pepper.

Amount per serving (2 total)

Timing Information:

Preparation	10 m
Cooking	15 m
Total Time	25 m

Nutritional Information:

Calories	203 kcal
Fat	18.9 g
Carbohydrates	6.3g
Protein	4.2 g
Cholesterol	50 mg
Sodium	214 mg

* Percent Daily Values are based on a 2,000 calorie diet.

HEAVY CREAM GRATIN SUPREME

Ingredients

- 1 lb. Brussels sprouts, cleaned and trimmed
- 2 slices turkey bacon, cut into 1/2 inch pieces
- salt and ground black pepper to taste
- 1/2 C. heavy cream
- 1/4 C. bread crumbs
- 1/4 C. grated Parmesan cheese
- 2 tbsp butter, cut into tiny pieces

Directions

- Set your oven to 400 degrees F before doing anything else and lightly, grease a baking dish.
- In a large pan of boiling water, cook the Brussels sprouts for about 8 minutes.
- Drain in a colander and then immediately immerse in ice water for several minutes to stop the cooking process.
- Then, drain well and cut in halves or quarters, depending on size and keep aside.
- Meanwhile, heat a large skillet on medium-high heat and cook the bacon for about 5 minutes.
- Reduce the heat and stir in the Brussels sprouts, salt and pepper and toss for about 1 minutes.

- Transfer the bacon and Brussels sprouts onto the prepared baking dish and top with the cream evenly.
- Sprinkle with the breadcrumbs and Parmesan cheese evenly.
- Spread the butter pieces over the bread crumbs.
- Cook in the oven for about 20-25 minutes.

Amount per serving (4 total)

Timing Information:

Preparation	15 m
Cooking	35 m
Total Time	1 h

Nutritional Information:

Calories	128 kcal
Fat	7.1 g
Carbohydrates	11.3g
Protein	7.3 g
Cholesterol	18 mg
Sodium	344 mg

* Percent Daily Values are based on a 2,000 calorie diet.

WEDNESDAY LUNCHEON BRUSSELS SPROUT

Ingredients

- 3 tbsp butter, divided
- 2 cloves garlic, chopped
- 2 C. broccoli florets
- 8 Brussels sprouts, trimmed and halved
- 1 small tomato, seeded and diced
- 1/4 tsp salt
- 1/8 tsp red pepper flakes

Directions

- In a skillet, melt 1 tbsp of the butter on medium heat and sauté the garlic for about 1-2 minutes.
- Stir in the broccoli and Brussels sprouts, tomato, remaining butter, salt and red pepper flakes and cook, covered for about 5 minutes.
- Flip sprouts and broccoli and cook, covered for about 4 minutes.

Amount per serving (4 total)

Timing Information:

Preparation	15 m
Cooking	10 m
Total Time	25 m

Nutritional Information:

Calories	128 kcal
Fat	7.1 g
Carbohydrates	11.3g
Protein	7.3 g
Cholesterol	18 mg
Sodium	344 mg

* Percent Daily Values are based on a 2,000 calorie diet.

Maryam's Brussels Sprouts

Ingredients

- 3 C. water
- 1 lb. Brussels sprouts, trimmed
- 2 tbsp olive oil
- 2 cloves garlic, minced
- 8 oz. pancetta bacon, diced
- 1 tsp salt
- 1 tsp ground black pepper

Directions

- In a large pan of boiling water, cook the Brussels sprouts for about 5-7 minutes.
- Drain, and rinse under the cold water.
- Then, slice the sprouts in half and keep aside.
- In a large skillet, heat 1 tbsp of the olive oil on medium-high heat and cook the garlic and pancetta for about 5 minutes.
- Add the remaining olive oil and Brussels sprouts and reduce the heat to medium.
- Cook, stirring till the sprouts are well coated with the flavor.

- Season with the salt and pepper and cook for about 5 minutes.

Amount per serving (4 total)

Timing Information:

Preparation	15 m
Cooking	20 m
Total Time	35 m

Nutritional Information:

Calories	369 kcal
Fat	32.3 g
Carbohydrates	11.4g
Protein	10.5 g
Cholesterol	38 mg
Sodium	1077 mg

* Percent Daily Values are based on a 2,000 calorie diet.

LOVEABLE BRUSSELS SPROUTS

Ingredients

- 1 tsp butter
- 1 tsp olive oil
- 12 Brussels sprouts, trimmed and thinly sliced
- 1 tbsp lemon juice
- salt and pepper to taste

Directions

- In a large skillet, heat the olive oil and butter on high heat and stir fry the Brussels sprouts and lemon juice for about 45 seconds.
- Season with the salt and pepper and serve.

Amount per serving (4 total)

Timing Information:

Preparation	5 m
Cooking	5 m
Total Time	10 m

Nutritional Information:

Calories	45 kcal
Fat	2.4 g
Carbohydrates	5.4g
Protein	2 g
Cholesterol	3 mg
Sodium	< 22 mg

* Percent Daily Values are based on a 2,000 calorie diet.

French Reverie Style Sprouts

Ingredients

- 1 tbsp butter
- 4 C. sliced Brussels sprouts
- 1 1/4 C. heavy cream
- 1/4 C. freshly shredded Parmesan cheese
- 1 clove garlic, minced
- salt and ground black pepper to taste
- 1 pinch ground nutmeg

Directions

- Set your oven to 300 degrees F before doing anything else and grease a 9x9-inch baking dish with the butter.
- Place the sliced Brussels sprouts into the prepared baking dish in an even layer.
- In a bowl, add the cream, Parmesan cheese, garlic, salt, and black pepper and beat till well combined.
- Place the cream mixture over the Brussels sprouts evenly and sprinkle with the nutmeg.
- With a piece of foil, cover the baking dish and cook in the oven for about 1 hour.
- Remove the piece of the foil and cook in the oven for about 15 minutes.

Amount per serving (8 total)

Timing Information:

Preparation	20 m
Cooking	1 h 15 m
Total Time	1 h 35 m

Nutritional Information:

Calories	172 kcal
Fat	16.1 g
Carbohydrates	5.3g
Protein	3.2 g
Cholesterol	57 mg
Sodium	78 mg

* Percent Daily Values are based on a 2,000 calorie diet.

Restaurant Pizza

Ingredients

- 1 tsp extra-virgin olive oil
- 9 slices pancetta
- 5 tsp extra-virgin olive oil
- 2 cloves garlic, minced
- 6 Brussels sprouts, trimmed and thinly sliced
- 1 (8 oz.) package shredded mozzarella cheese
- 1/2 tsp fennel seed
- 1 12-inch pizza crust

Directions

- Set your oven to 475 degrees F before doing anything else.
- In a skillet, heat 1 tsp of the olive oil on medium heat and cook the pancetta for about 3-5 minutes.
- Transfer the pancetta onto a paper towel-lined plate to drain.
- Then crumble the pancetta.
- In the same skillet, heat the remaining 5 tsp of the olive oil and sauté the garlic for about 20 seconds.
- Add the Brussels sprouts and cook, stirring continuously for about 5-10 minutes.

- Transfer the sprouts and garlic into a bowl with the crumbled pancetta, mozzarella cheese and fennel seed and toss to coat.
- Arrange the pizza crust onto a baking sheet and top with the Brussels sprouts mixture evenly.
- Cook in the oven for about 10 minutes.

Amount per serving (4 total)

Timing Information:

Preparation	10 m
Cooking	20 m
Total Time	30 m

Nutritional Information:

Calories	520 kcal
Fat	27.2 g
Carbohydrates	38.8g
Protein	28.6 g
Cholesterol	59 mg
Sodium	1309 mg

* Percent Daily Values are based on a 2,000 calorie diet.

Gourmet Brussels Sprouts

Ingredients

- 1 (16 oz.) package fresh Brussels sprouts
- 1 small red onion, thinly sliced
- 5 tbsp olive oil, divided
- 1/4 tsp salt
- 1/4 tsp freshly ground black pepper
- 1 shallot, chopped
- 1/4 C. balsamic vinegar
- 1 tbsp chopped fresh rosemary

Directions

- Set your oven to 425 degrees F before doing anything else and lightly, grease a baking sheet.
- In a bowl, add the Brussels sprouts, onion, 3 tbsp of the olive oil, salt and pepper and gently toss to coat.
- Transfer the sprouts mixture onto the prepared baking sheet.
- Cook in the oven for about 25-30 minutes.
- In a small skillet, heat the remaining 2 tbsp of the olive oil on medium-high heat and sauté the shallot for about 5 minutes.
- Add the balsamic vinegar and cook for about 5 minutes.

- Stir in the rosemary and pour the glaze over the sprouts mixture.

Amount per serving (6 total)

Timing Information:

Preparation	10 m
Cooking	35 m
Total Time	45 m

Nutritional Information:

Calories	150 kcal
Fat	11.5 g
Carbohydrates	10.9g
Protein	3 g
Cholesterol	0 mg
Sodium	120 mg

* Percent Daily Values are based on a 2,000 calorie diet.

NUTTY SPROUTS

Ingredients

- 4 lb. Brussels sprouts
- 1/2 C. unsalted butter
- 4 small red onions, cut into strips
- 1/4 C. red wine vinegar
- 2 tbsp white sugar
- salt and pepper to taste
- 1/2 C. coarsely chopped pistachios

Directions

- Arrange a steamer basket in a pan of the boiling water.
- Place the Brussels sprouts in the steamer basket and cook, covered for about 8-10 minutes.
- In a deep skillet, melt the butter on medium heat and cook the onions and 3 tbsp of the vinegar till the onions are browned.
- Add the Brussels sprouts, sugar and remaining vinegar and sauté till the Brussels sprouts are lightly caramelized.
- Season with the salt and pepper and remove from the heat.
- Serve with a garnishing of the pistachios.

Amount per serving (8 total)

Timing Information:

Preparation	15 m
Cooking	30 m
Total Time	1 h 20 m

Nutritional Information:

Calories	271 kcal
Fat	15.9 g
Carbohydrates	28.9g
Protein	9.9 g
Cholesterol	31 mg
Sodium	93 mg

* Percent Daily Values are based on a 2,000 calorie diet.

CARAMELIZED BRUSSELS SPROUTS

Ingredients

- 10 Brussels sprouts, halved
- 1 1/2 tsp butter, melted
- 1 1/2 tsp honey
- 1/2 tsp Dijon mustard
- 1 pinch dried dill weed
- 1 pinch onion powder

Directions

- In a large pan of lightly salted boiling water, cook the Brussels sprouts for about 8-10 minutes.
- Drain well and transfer into a large bowl.
- Add the butter, honey, Dijon mustard, dill weed and onion powder and toss to coat.

Amount per serving (2 total)

Timing Information:

Preparation	5 m
Cooking	10 m
Total Time	15 m

Nutritional Information:

Calories	89 kcal
Fat	3.4 g
Carbohydrates	14.1g
Protein	3.4 g
Cholesterol	8 mg
Sodium	78 mg

* Percent Daily Values are based on a 2,000 calorie diet.

CLASSICAL VEGGIE COMBO

Ingredients

- 1/3 C. balsamic vinaigrette salad dressing (such as Kraft(R))
- 1 tbsp brown sugar
- 1 tbsp chopped fresh thyme
- 1 lb. Brussels sprouts, halved
- 1 lb. parsnips, peeled
- 1 large red onion, thickly sliced

Directions

- Set your oven to 400 degrees F before doing anything else.
- In a bowl, mix together the salad dressing, brown sugar and thyme.
- In a 13x9-inch baking dish, add the Brussels sprouts, parsnips, red onion and dressing mixture and toss to coat.
- Cook in the oven for about 40 minutes.

Amount per serving (4 total)

Timing Information:

Preparation	15 m
Cooking	40 m
Total Time	55 m

Nutritional Information:

Calories	222 kcal
Fat	6.7 g
Carbohydrates	39.6g
Protein	5.6 g
Cholesterol	0 mg
Sodium	276 mg

* Percent Daily Values are based on a 2,000 calorie diet.

Sunday Hash

Ingredients

- 1/4 C. honey-flavored butter
- 1/2 C. chopped onion
- 1 lb. Brussels sprouts, grated
- salt and ground black pepper to taste
- 2 tbsp white cooking wine

Directions

- In a large skillet, melt the honey-flavored butter on medium-high heat and sauté the onion for about 5-7 minutes.
- Add the Brussels sprouts, salt and pepper. Sauté sprouts and sauté for about 5-7 minutes.
- Remove the skillet from the heat and drizzle with the wine and toss to coat.

Amount per serving (4 total)

Timing Information:

Preparation	10 m
Cooking	20 m
Total Time	30 m

Nutritional Information:

Calories	152 kcal
Fat	8.4 g
Carbohydrates	16.9g
Protein	4.1 g
Cholesterol	15 mg
Sodium	206 mg

* Percent Daily Values are based on a 2,000 calorie diet.

COOK OUT BBQ BRUSSELS SPROUTS

Ingredients

- 2 tbsp melted butter
- 1 (16 oz.) package Brussels sprouts, halved
- 2 tsp garlic powder
- 2 tsp cracked black pepper
- 1 pinch seasoned salt
- 1 lime, halved

Directions

- Set your grill for medium-high heat and lightly, grease the grill grate.
- Coat the Brussels sprouts with the melted butter and season with the garlic powder, black pepper and seasoned salt.
- Cook the Brussels sprouts on the grill for about 10 minutes.
- Drizzle the Brussels sprouts with the lime juice before removing from the grill.

Amount per serving (8 total)

Timing Information:

Preparation	10 m
Cooking	10 m
Total Time	20 m

Nutritional Information:

Calories	55 kcal
Fat	3.1 g
Carbohydrates	6.4g
Protein	2.1 g
Cholesterol	8 mg
Sodium	64 mg

* Percent Daily Values are based on a 2,000 calorie diet.

5 Ingredient Snack

Ingredients

- 2 tbsp olive oil
- 1 1/2 tsp Dijon mustard
- 1/4 tsp sea salt
- 1 pinch red pepper flakes
- 1 lb. Brussels sprouts

Directions

- Set your oven to 325 degrees F before doing anything else and arrange a rack in the top third of the oven.
- Line a baking sheet with a piece of the foil.
- For sauce in a bowl, mix together the olive oil, Dijon mustard, sea salt and red pepper flakes.
- Trim the stems of the Brussels sprouts to remove the outermost leaves, about 5 leaves from each sprout.
- Add the leaves in the bowl of sauce and with your fingers, mix till all the leaves are coated evenly.
- Spread the leaves onto the prepared baking sheet in a single layer.
- Cook in the oven for about 15 minutes.

- Transfer any crispy leaves onto a serving plate and cook in the oven, removing crispy leaves at 5-minute intervals, for about 10 minutes.

Amount per serving (4 total)

Timing Information:

Preparation	15 m
Cooking	25 m
Total Time	40 m

Nutritional Information:

Calories	111 kcal
Fat	7.1 g
Carbohydrates	10.7g
Protein	3.9 g
Cholesterol	0 mg
Sodium	185 mg

* Percent Daily Values are based on a 2,000 calorie diet.

Rustic Green Bean, Turnip, and Leeks Soup

Ingredients

- 12 C. chicken broth
- 1 C. chopped fresh green beans
- 1 1/4 C. cubed turnips
- 1/2 C. chopped leeks
- 1/2 C. chopped carrots
- 1/3 C. barley
- 1 1/2 lb. Brussels sprouts, trimmed and cut in half
- 1/2 C. chopped green bell pepper
- 1 tsp salt
- 1/2 tsp ground black pepper
- 1/4 C. butter
- 1/2 C. all-purpose flour

Directions

- In a large soup pan, add the chicken broth and bring to a boil on medium-high heat.
- Add the beans, turnips, leeks, carrots and barley and reduce the heat to medium.
- Simmer for about 30 minutes.

- Add the Brussels sprouts, green pepper, salt and pepper and simmer for about 30 minutes.
- In a small frying pan, melt the butter on medium heat and cook the flour, beating continuously till smooth.
- Stir the flour mixture into the soup and simmer for about 10 minutes.

Amount per serving (12 total)

Timing Information:

Preparation	25 m
Cooking	1 h 10 m
Total Time	1 h 35 m

Nutritional Information:

Calories	146 kcal
Fat	5.6 g
Carbohydrates	16.6g
Protein	8.4 g
Cholesterol	10 mg
Sodium	1013 mg

* Percent Daily Values are based on a 2,000 calorie diet.

VENICE BRUSSELS SPROUTS

Ingredients

- 1 lb. Brussels sprouts, trimmed
- 6 sprigs fresh parsley, finely chopped
- 2 tsp lemon zest
- 1 clove garlic, thickly sliced
- 2 tbsp butter, melted
- salt and ground black pepper to taste

Directions

- In a large pan of boiling water, cook the Brussels sprouts for about 5 minutes, stirring occasionally.
- Drain well and transfer into a bowl.
- In a small bowl, mix together the parsley, lemon zest and garlic.
- Add the butter, parsley mixture, salt and black pepper in the bowl with the Brussels sprouts and gently, toss to coat.

Amount per serving (4 total)

Timing Information:

Preparation	15 m
Cooking	5 m
Total Time	20 m

Nutritional Information:

Calories	116 kcal
Fat	6.4 g
Carbohydrates	13.2g
Protein	5.2 g
Cholesterol	15 mg
Sodium	93 mg

* Percent Daily Values are based on a 2,000 calorie diet.

NORTH INDIAN INSPIRED BRUSSELS SPROUT

Ingredients

- 1 (16 oz.) package Brussels sprouts
- 1 C. chickpea flour
- 3 tbsp rice flour
- 1 tbsp ground coriander
- 1 tsp ground cumin
- 1/2 tsp baking powder
- salt and ground black pepper to taste
- 1 C. water, or more as needed
- 1/2 C. chopped fresh cilantro
- 2 chili peppers, seeded and diced
- vegetable oil for frying

Directions

- Arrange a steamer basket in a pan of the boiling water.
- Place the Brussels sprouts in the steamer basket and cook, covered for about 5 minutes.
- In a large bowl, sift together the chickpea and rice flour.
- Add the coriander, cumin, baking powder, salt and black pepper and mix.

- Add enough water and beat till the pancake mixture like mixture forms.
- In a deep-fryer, heat the oil to 350 degrees F.
- Place the mixture by a few tbsp at a time into the hot oil and fry for about 5 minutes.

Amount per serving (4 total)

Timing Information:

Preparation	15 m
Cooking	10 m
Total Time	25 m

Nutritional Information:

Calories	374 kcal
Fat	24.4 g
Carbohydrates	33.4g
Protein	9.8 g
Cholesterol	0 mg
Sodium	135 mg

* Percent Daily Values are based on a 2,000 calorie diet.

BRUSSELS SPROUTS STIR FRY

Ingredients

- 1/2 tsp butter
- 3 Brussels sprouts, trimmed, halved lengthwise, and thinly sliced
- 2 1/2 tsp chopped dried apricots
- 1 tsp water
- 3/4 tsp maple syrup
- 1 tsp lime juice

Directions

- In a skillet, melt the butter on medium-high heat and sauté the sprouts, apricot, water and maple syrup for about 5-10 minutes.
- Stir in the lime juice and immediately remove from the heat.

Amount per serving (1 total)

Timing Information:

Preparation	15 m
Cooking	5 m
Total Time	20 m

Nutritional Information:

Calories	73 kcal
Fat	2.2 g
Carbohydrates	13.1g
Protein	2.2 g
Cholesterol	5 mg
Sodium	30 mg

* Percent Daily Values are based on a 2,000 calorie diet.

PANHANDLE BRUSSELS SPROUTS

Ingredients

- 1 1/2 lb. Brussels sprouts
- 3 tbsp extra-virgin olive oil
- 1 tsp red pepper flakes
- salt and ground black pepper to taste
- 1 small red onion, chopped
- 3 cloves garlic, coarsely chopped
- 2 tbsp butter

Directions

- In a large pan of lightly salted boiling water, cook the Brussels sprouts for about 1-2 minutes.
- Drain well and run sprouts under cold water to stop the cooking process.
- Trim the ends of Brussels sprouts and slice in half.
- In a large skillet, heat the olive oil on medium heat and place the Brussels sprouts, cut sides down with the red pepper flakes, salt and black pepper.
- Cook for about 7-9 minutes, without stirring.
- In a cold saucepan; place sauce Stir in the red onion and garlic and cook for about 10-13 minutes.

- In a pan, melt the butter on medium heat for about 5 minutes.
- Reduce the heat to low and brown the butter for about 5-10 minutes, stirring continuously.
- Remove from the heat and place the browned butter over Brussels sprouts and toss to coat.
- Keep aside.

Amount per serving (6 total)

Timing Information:

Preparation	15 m
Cooking	30 m
Total Time	45 m

Nutritional Information:

Calories	152 kcal
Fat	11 g
Carbohydrates	12g
Protein	4.2 g
Cholesterol	10 mg
Sodium	57 mg

* Percent Daily Values are based on a 2,000 calorie diet.

ORIENTAL BRUSSELS SPROUTS

Ingredients

- 1/2 lb. Brussels sprouts
- 1 tbsp olive oil
- 1/4 C. chopped pecans
- 1/4 C. orange juice
- 1/2 C. dried cranberries
- 1 tbsp freshly grated ginger

Directions

- In a food processor, add the Brussels sprouts and pulse till shredded.
- In a skillet, heat the olive oil on medium heat and cook the shredded Brussels sprouts for about 5 minutes.
- Reduce the heat to low and stir fry the pecans for about 2 minutes.
- Stir in the orange juice, cranberries and ginger and simmer for about 5 minutes.

Amount per serving (4 total)

Timing Information:

Preparation	10 m
Cooking	15 m
Total Time	25 m

Nutritional Information:

Calories	154 kcal
Fat	8.5 g
Carbohydrates	20.3g
Protein	2.7 g
Cholesterol	0 mg
Sodium	15 mg

* Percent Daily Values are based on a 2,000 calorie diet.

SUNFLOWER AND CRANBERRY SALAD

Ingredients

- 1 shallot, minced
- 1/4 C. cider vinegar
- 1/4 C. sunflower seed oil
- 2 tbsp Dijon mustard
- 1/2 tsp honey
- 1/2 tsp salt
- 1/4 tsp ground black pepper
- 6 C. Brussels sprouts, trimmed, halved, and sliced
- 2 Gala apples, cored and thinly sliced
- 1/2 C. dried cranberries
- 1/3 C. sliced almonds
- 1/3 C. raw sunflower seed kernels
- 1/3 C. shelled, raw pumpkin seeds

Directions

- In a bowl, add the shallot, vinegar, oil, Dijon mustard, honey, salt and pepper and beat till well combined.
- In another large bowl, mix together the Brussels sprouts, apples, cranberries, almonds, sunflower seeds, and pumpkin seeds in a bowl; pour vinegar mixture over and toss to combine.

Amount per serving (8 total)

Timing Information:

Preparation	
Cooking	20 m
Total Time	20 m

Nutritional Information:

Calories	230 kcal
Fat	14.8 g
Carbohydrates	22.2g
Protein	6 g
Cholesterol	0 mg
Sodium	259 mg

* Percent Daily Values are based on a 2,000 calorie diet.

Saint Anne's Meal

Ingredients

- 1 lb. fresh chestnuts
- 1 lb. Brussels sprouts, halved
- 3 tbsp butter
- 2 shallots, minced
- salt and ground black pepper to taste
- 1 pinch ground nutmeg

Directions

- Score the flat side of all chestnuts with an X.
- In a large pan of water, add the chestnuts and bring to a boil.
- Cook for about 10 minutes.
- With a slotted spoon, transfer the chestnuts in a bowl and keep aside to cool slightly.
- Peel the outer shell and brown skin.
- Return the chestnuts into the pan on medium heat and boil for about 20-25 minutes.
- Drain and keep aside.
- Meanwhile in a large pan of lightly salted boiling water, cook the Brussels sprouts for about 7-10 minutes.

- Drain in a colander and immediately immerse in the ice water for several minutes to stop the cooking process.
- After cooling, drain well and keep aside.
- In a skillet, melt the butter on medium heat and sauté the shallots for about 5 minutes.
- Stir in the chestnuts, Brussels sprouts, salt, pepper and nutmeg and cook for about 5 minutes.

Amount per serving (8 total)

Timing Information:

Preparation	20 m
Cooking	40 m
Total Time	1 h

Nutritional Information:

Calories	183 kcal
Fat	5.3 g
Carbohydrates	32.3g
Protein	3.2 g
Cholesterol	11 mg
Sodium	96 mg

* Percent Daily Values are based on a 2,000 calorie diet.

BRUSSELS SPROUTS SALAD

Ingredients

Dressing:

- 1/4 C. olive oil
- 2 tbsp distilled white vinegar
- 1 tbsp honey
- 1 clove garlic, minced
- 1 tsp brown mustard

Salad:

- 1 lb. Brussels sprouts, shredded
- 1/2 C. dried cherries
- 1/2 C. slivered almonds
- 1/2 C. grated Parmesan cheese

Directions

- In a bowl, add the olive oil, vinegar, honey, garlic and mustard and beat till a smooth dressing is formed.
- In another large bowl, add the Brussels sprouts, dried cherries, almonds, and Parmesan cheese.
- Add the dressing and toss to coat.

Amount per serving (6 total)

Timing Information:

Preparation	
Cooking	20 m
Total Time	20 m

Nutritional Information:

Calories	248 kcal
Fat	15.8 g
Carbohydrates	20.6g
Protein	7.8 g
Cholesterol	6 mg
Sodium	135 mg

* Percent Daily Values are based on a 2,000 calorie diet.

3 INGREDIENT BRUSSELS SPROUTS

Ingredients

- 20 Brussels sprouts, cleaned and trimmed
- 2 tbsp butter, melted
- 1 C. Italian seasoned dry bread crumbs

Directions

- In a large pan of boiling water, cook the Brussels sprouts, covered for about 15-20 minutes.
- Drain well and keep aside to dry for a few minutes.
- In a serving bowl, place the Brussels sprouts and melted butter and toss to coat.
- Add the breadcrumbs and gently, stir to combine.

Amount per serving (4 total)

Timing Information:

Preparation	10 m
Cooking	20 m
Total Time	30 m

Nutritional Information:

Calories	202 kcal
Fat	7.5 g
Carbohydrates	28.5g
Protein	7.3 g
Cholesterol	15 mg
Sodium	495 mg

* Percent Daily Values are based on a 2,000 calorie diet.

THANKSGIVING BRUSSELS SPROUTS

Ingredients

- 1 C. water
- 2 (10 oz.) packages frozen Brussels sprouts
- 1/4 C. butter
- 8 oz. walnuts
- 3 tbsp firmly packed brown sugar
- 1/4 tsp ground allspice
- 1/4 tsp ground nutmeg
- 1/4 tsp salt

Directions

- In a large pan of boiling water, cook the Brussels sprouts, covered for about 5-7 minutes.
- Drain well.
- In a microwave safe bowl, mix together the butter, walnuts, brown sugar, allspice, nutmeg and salt microwave on High, covered for about 3-4 minutes, stirring occasionally.
- Place the butter mixture over the cooked Brussels sprouts and lightly, toss to coat.
- Serve immediately.

Amount per serving (7 total)

Timing Information:

Preparation	10 m
Cooking	11 m
Total Time	25 m

Nutritional Information:

Calories	326 kcal
Fat	28.1 g
Carbohydrates	16.6g
Protein	8.1 g
Cholesterol	17 mg
Sodium	140 mg

* Percent Daily Values are based on a 2,000 calorie diet.

CAROLINA STYLE BRUSSELS SPROUTS

Ingredients

- 3 C. Brussels sprouts
- 1 C. chestnuts, peeled
- 1 large oranges, peeled and segmented
- 1/2 C. low fat, low sodium chicken broth
- 1 tbsp canola oil
- salt and pepper to taste

Directions

- Set your oven to 350 degrees F before doing anything else.
- Trim the Brussels sprout by cutting a little piece off the bottom.
- With a small paring knife, make an X in the top of all the Brussels sprout.
- Arrange a steamer basket in a pan of the boiling water.
- Place the Brussels sprouts in the steamer basket and cook, covered for about 10 minutes.
- Drain well and keep aside to cool.
- Cut the Brussels sprout in half and place in a casserole dish.
- Top with the chestnuts, followed by the oranges.
- Pour the broth over all ingredients evenly.

- Drizzle with the oil and sprinkle with the pepper and salt.
- Cook in the oven for about 15 minutes.

Amount per serving (6 total)

Timing Information:

Preparation	20 m
Cooking	40 m
Total Time	1 h 10 m

Nutritional Information:

Calories	102 kcal
Fat	2.8 g
Carbohydrates	18.2g
Protein	2.4 g
Cholesterol	0 mg
Sodium	44 mg

* Percent Daily Values are based on a 2,000 calorie diet.

Sprout Lover's Platter

Ingredients

- 1/4 C. butter
- 1 1/2 lb. Brussels sprouts, trimmed and quartered
- 1/4 tsp sea salt
- 1 C. heavy cream
- 2 tbsp fresh lemon juice

Directions

- In a skillet, melt the butter on medium-high heat and cook the Brussels sprouts and salt for about 5 minutes, stirring occasionally.
- Add the cream and bring to a simmer.
- Reduce the heat to low and simmer, covered for about 30-35 minutes.
- Uncover and stir in the lemon juice.
- Simmer for a few minutes more.
- Season with the additional salt and lemon juice before serving.

Amount per serving (6 total)

Timing Information:

Preparation	10 m
Cooking	40 m
Total Time	50 m

Nutritional Information:

Calories	255 kcal
Fat	22.7 g
Carbohydrates	11.7g
Protein	4.7 g
Cholesterol	75 mg
Sodium	171 mg

* Percent Daily Values are based on a 2,000 calorie diet.

PLAY BALL BRUSSELS SPROUTS

Ingredients

- 2 tbsp olive oil
- 1 onion, chopped
- 8 beef frankfurters, sliced
- 1 clove garlic, minced
- 1 C. spicy vegetable juice cocktail
- 1 tsp Worcestershire sauce
- 1 large tomato, chopped
- 3 C. Brussels sprouts, halved
- freshly ground black pepper to ta

Directions

- In a large skillet, heat the olive oil on medium heat and sauté the onion till tender.
- Add the sliced frankfurters and cook till browned slightly.
- Stir in the garlic and cook for about 30 seconds.
- Stir in the vegetable juice cocktail, Worcestershire sauce, tomato, Brussels sprouts and pepper on low heat and simmer, covered for about 15-20 minutes.

Amount per serving (4 total)

Timing Information:

Preparation	30 m
Cooking	30 m
Total Time	1 h

Nutritional Information:

Calories	419 kcal
Fat	33.7 g
Carbohydrates	17.4g
Protein	13.5 g
Cholesterol	48 mg
Sodium	1223 mg

* Percent Daily Values are based on a 2,000 calorie diet.

POTATO AND BRUSSELS SPROUTS SKILLET

Ingredients

- 1 tbsp vegetable oil
- 1 onion, chopped
- 1 large potato, peeled and cubed
- 1 bay leaf
- 1 lb. Brussels sprouts, trimmed and halved lengthwise
- 1 red pepper, seeded and cut into 1/2-inch cubes
- 1/4 C. chicken broth
- ground black pepper, to taste
- 2 tbsp chopped green onions

Directions

- In a skillet, heat the vegetable oil on medium heat and stir fry the onion, potato and bay leaf for about 5 minutes.
- Add the Brussels sprouts, red pepper and chicken broth and cook, covered for about 10 minutes.
- Discard the bay leaf.
- Season with the black pepper.
- Serve immediately with a garnishing of the green onions.

Amount per serving (8 total)

Timing Information:

Preparation	20 m
Cooking	15 m
Total Time	35 m

Nutritional Information:

Calories	86 kcal
Fat	2 g
Carbohydrates	15.5g
Protein	3.2 g
Cholesterol	0 mg
Sodium	18 mg

* Percent Daily Values are based on a 2,000 calorie diet.

November's Brussels Sprouts Casserole

Ingredients

- 1 bulb garlic
- 2 tbsp olive oil
- 1 lb. Brussels sprouts, trimmed and halved
- 1/3 C. diced prosciutto
- 1/3 C. sweetened dried cranberries (such as Ocean Spray(R) Craisins(R))
- 3 tbsp olive oil
- 1/4 C. low-sodium chicken broth
- 1/4 C. balsamic vinegar
- kosher salt to taste
- freshly ground black pepper to taste

Directions

- Set your oven to 350 degrees F before doing anything else.
- Slice off the top part of the garlic bulb and place in an oven-safe ramekin.
- Drizzle the garlic bulb with 2 tbsp of the olive oil.
- With a piece of the ramekin, cover the ramekin and cook in the oven for about 30-45 minutes.

- Remove from the oven and keep aside to cool.
- In a 13x9--inch baking dish, place the Brussels sprouts, prosciutto, cranberries, 3 tbsp of the olive oil, chicken broth, balsamic vinegar, salt and black pepper and toss to coat well.
- Squeeze the roasted garlic cloves into a small bowl and mash slightly.
- Add the mashed garlic into the Brussels sprouts mixture and mix well.
- Cook in the oven for about 30 minutes.

Amount per serving (4 total)

Timing Information:

Preparation	20 m
Cooking	1 h
Total Time	1 h 20 m

Nutritional Information:

Calories	303 kcal
Fat	21 g
Carbohydrates	25.6g
Protein	7.2 g
Cholesterol	10 mg
Sodium	1703 mg

* Percent Daily Values are based on a 2,000 calorie diet.

Monday's Brussels Sprout Appetizer

Ingredients

- 2 lb. Brussels sprouts
- 2 quarts water
- 1/2 C. kosher salt
- 1/2 C. sugar
- 1/4 C. Kikkoman Soy Sauce*
- 3 tbsp olive oil
- 1 tsp black pepper

Directions

- Trim the stems of the Brussels sprouts and discard the wilted leaves.
- Rinse the Brussels sprouts under cold water.
- In a large bowl, add the water, salt, sugar and soy sauce and stir till the sugar is dissolved.
- Add the Brussels sprouts and brine for about 1 hour.
- Set your oven to 400 degrees F.
- Drain the Brussels sprouts and transfer into a baking dish.
- Add the olive oil and black pepper and toss to coat.

- Cook in the oven for about 35-40 minutes.

Amount per serving (10 total)

Timing Information:

Preparation	10 m
Cooking	1 h 20 m
Total Time	1 h 30 m

Nutritional Information:

Calories	118 kcal
Fat	4.3 g
Carbohydrates	18.3g
Protein	3.9 g
Cholesterol	0 mg
Sodium	4951 mg

* Percent Daily Values are based on a 2,000 calorie diet.

BRUSSELS SPROUTS FOR JULY

Ingredients

- 1/4 C. low-sodium teriyaki sauce
- 1 tbsp sesame oil
- 1 tsp smoked paprika
- 1 tsp garlic powder
- 1 tbsp olive oil
- 2 cloves garlic, minced
- 10 Brussels sprouts, halved
- 1 tsp ground black pepper

Directions

- In a bowl, add the teriyaki sauce, sesame oil, paprika, and garlic powder and beat till well combined.
- In a non-stick skillet, heat the olive oil on medium heat and sauté the garlic for about 2 minutes.
- Add the Brussels sprouts, cut-side down and sprinkle with the pepper.
- Place about 1/3 of the teriyaki mixture over the Brussels sprouts and cook for about 5-10 minutes, coating the Brussels sprouts with the teriyaki mixture 2 more times.

Amount per serving (3 total)

Timing Information:

Preparation	10 m
Cooking	10 m
Total Time	20 m

Nutritional Information:

Calories	130 kcal
Fat	9.4 g
Carbohydrates	10.6g
Protein	2.6 g
Cholesterol	0 mg
Sodium	364 mg

* Percent Daily Values are based on a 2,000 calorie diet.

Extra Virgin Brussels Sprouts

Ingredients

- 1 tbsp extra-virgin olive oil
- 1/2 C. finely chopped onion
- 1 lb. Brussels sprouts, trimmed
- 1/2 C. sour cream
- 2 tbsp bacon bits
- 1 tbsp unsalted butter
- 1 dash hot sauce
- salt to taste

Directions

- Arrange a steamer basket in a pan of the boiling water.
- Place the Brussels sprouts in the steamer basket and cook, covered for about 10-15 minutes.
- Meanwhile in a skillet, heat the olive oil on medium heat and sauté the onion for about 2-3 minutes.
- Transfer the onion into a large bowl.
- Drain the Brussels sprouts and transfer into the same bowl with the onion.
- Add the sour cream, bacon bits, butter, hot sauce and salt and gently, stir to combine.

Amount per serving (4 total)

Timing Information:

Preparation	10 m
Cooking	15 m
Total Time	25 m

Nutritional Information:

Calories	187 kcal
Fat	13.4 g
Carbohydrates	13.4g
Protein	6.5 g
Cholesterol	23 mg
Sodium	258 mg

* Percent Daily Values are based on a 2,000 calorie diet.

3-INGREDIENT BRUSSELS SPROUTS

Ingredients

- 1 lb. Brussels sprouts, trimmed
- 1 (16 oz.) bottle zesty Italian-style salad dressing
- 3 dashes hot sauce

Directions

- In a large pan of lightly salted boiling water, cook the Brussels sprouts for about 15 minutes, stirring occasionally.
- Drain well and transfer into a large bowl with the Italian dressing and hot sauce and toss to coat.
- Refrigerate to marinate for about 4 hours, stirring occasionally.

Amount per serving (6 total)

Timing Information:

Preparation	10 m
Cooking	15 m
Total Time	4 h 25 m

Nutritional Information:

Calories	247 kcal
Fat	21.1 g
Carbohydrates	14.5g
Protein	2.8 g
Cholesterol	0 mg
Sodium	1252 mg

* Percent Daily Values are based on a 2,000 calorie diet.

EL SAHA BRUSSELS SPROUTS

Ingredients

- 1 2/3 lb. Brussels sprouts, trimmed
- 1 lb. carrots, cut into 1-inch pieces
- 2 tbsp butter
- 2 tbsp chopped onion
- 1 (10.5 oz.) can condensed beef consommé (such as Campbell's(R))
- 1/3 C. apple juice
- 2 tbsp cornstarch
- 2 tsp lemon juice
- 1 tbsp brown sugar
- 2 pinches ground cloves

Directions

- In a large pan of lightly salted boiling water, cook the Brussels sprouts and carrots for about 8-10 minutes.
- Drain well.
- In a pan, melt the butter on medium heat and sauté the onion for about 5 minutes.
- Add the beef consommé, apple juice, cornstarch, lemon juice, brown sugar and cloves and cook for about 5 minutes, stirring occasionally.

- Fold in the Brussels sprouts and carrots.

Amount per serving (8 total)

Timing Information:

Preparation	15 m
Cooking	20 m
Total Time	35 m

Nutritional Information:

Calories	113 kcal
Fat	3.4 g
Carbohydrates	19.1g
Protein	4.2 g
Cholesterol	8 mg
Sodium	206 mg

* Percent Daily Values are based on a 2,000 calorie diet.

ACROPOLIS BRUSSELS SPROUTS

Ingredients

- 1 1/2 lb. Brussels sprouts
- 1 tsp salt
- 4 tbsp butter, melted
- 4 tbsp grated Parmesan cheese
- 4 tbsp dried bread crumbs
- 1/4 tsp garlic powder
- 1/4 tsp ground black pepper
- 1/4 tsp seasoning salt

Directions

- Set the broiler of your oven and arrange oven rack about 4-inches from the heating element.
- Wash and trim the Brussels sprouts completely.
- Cut an "X" about 1/8-inch deep in the stem of each Brussels sprout.
- In a medium pan of the water, add the Brussels sprouts and 1 tsp of the salt and bring to boil.
- Simmer, covered for about 6 minutes.
- Transfer the Brussels sprouts in a small casserole dish with 2 tbsp of the melted butter and toss to coat.

- In a bowl, add the Parmesan cheese, dried bread crumbs, garlic powder, black pepper, seasoning salt and remaining butter and mix till well combined.
- Spread the cheese mixture over the Brussels sprouts evenly.
- Cook under the broiler for about 5 minutes.
- Serve hot.

Amount per serving (8 total)

Timing Information:

Preparation	25 m
Cooking	12 m
Total Time	37 m

Nutritional Information:

Calories	112 kcal
Fat	6.9 g
Carbohydrates	10.3g
Protein	4.4 g
Cholesterol	17 mg
Sodium	444 mg

* Percent Daily Values are based on a 2,000 calorie diet.

ATHENIAN CITY STATE BRUSSELS SPROUTS

Ingredients

- 1 1/2 lb. Brussels sprouts, trimmed
- 2 tbsp olive oil
- 1 onion, thinly sliced
- 2 cloves garlic, minced
- 1/4 C. balsamic vinegar
- 2 tbsp butter
- 1 tsp salt
- 1/2 tsp ground black pepper
- 1/2 tsp garlic powder

Directions

- In a large pan of lightly salted boiling water, cook the Brussels sprouts for about 2 minutes.
- Drain well and immediately, immerse in ice water for several minutes to stop the cooking process.
- Drain well.
- In a skillet, heat the olive oil on medium heat and sauté the onion and garlic for about 5-10 minutes.

- Add the Brussels sprouts and cook for about 8-10 minutes.
- Add the balsamic vinegar, butter, salt, black pepper and garlic powder and toss to coat.

Amount per serving (6 total)

Timing Information:

Preparation	10 m
Cooking	15 m
Total Time	25 m

Nutritional Information:

Calories	147 kcal
Fat	8.8 g
Carbohydrates	15.9g
Protein	4.5 g
Cholesterol	10 mg
Sodium	448 mg

* Percent Daily Values are based on a 2,000 calorie diet.

Lunch Box Brussels Sprouts

Ingredients

- 4 C. Brussels sprouts, trimmed and halved
- 1/2 lb. whole mushrooms
- 5 tbsp butter
- 1/2 C. chopped fresh parsley
- salt and pepper to taste
- fresh lemon juice

Directions

- In a large pan of lightly salted boiling water, cook the Brussels sprouts, covered for about 15 minutes.
- Drain well and keep aside.
- In a large skillet, melt the butter on medium-high heat and cook the mushrooms till browned lightly.
- Add the Brussels sprouts and lemon juice and toss to coat.
- Serve immediately with a sprinkling of the parsley.

Amount per serving (6 total)

Timing Information:

Preparation	15 m
Cooking	25 m
Total Time	40 m

Nutritional Information:

Calories	119 kcal
Fat	10.1 g
Carbohydrates	7.3g
Protein	2.5 g
Cholesterol	25 mg
Sodium	472 mg

* Percent Daily Values are based on a 2,000 calorie diet.

Swiss Mushroom Dinner

Ingredients

- 1 tbsp olive oil
- 4 skinless, boneless chicken breast halves
- 1/2 C. water
- 20 Brussels sprouts, halved
- 1 (4 oz.) package sliced fresh mushrooms
- 2 C. shredded Swiss cheese
- 1 pint half-and-half
- 3/4 C. milk
- 3 cloves garlic, chopped
- freshly ground black pepper to taste
- garlic salt to taste
- 1/4 C. grated Parmesan cheese (optional)

Directions

- Set your oven to 400 degrees F before doing anything else and lightly, grease a 13x9-inch baking dish.
- In a skillet, heat the olive oil on medium heat and cook the chicken for about 5 minutes per side.
- Remove from the heat and cut into strips.
- In a large pan of lightly salted boiling water, cook the Brussels sprouts, covered for about 10 minutes.

- Drain well and place the Brussels sprouts in the prepared baking dish.
- Place the mushrooms over the sprouts and sprinkle with 1 C. of the Swiss cheese evenly.
- Top with the chicken strips evenly.
- In a bowl, add the half-and-half, milk, garlic and remaining Swiss cheese and mix till well combined.
- Place the milk mixture over the chicken and sprinkle with the pepper and garlic salt.
- Cook in the oven, covered for about 35 minutes.
- Now, set your oven to 350 degrees F.
- Remove the cover and cook in the oven for about 20 minutes.
- Serve with a sprinkling of the Parmesan cheese.

Amount per serving (6 total)

Timing Information:

Preparation	15 m
Cooking	1 h 10 m
Total Time	1 h 25 m

Nutritional Information:

Calories	601 kcal
Fat	39.3 g
Carbohydrates	16.9g
Protein	46.1 g
Cholesterol	159 mg
Sodium	369 mg

* Percent Daily Values are based on a 2,000 calorie diet.

BACKROAD BRUSSEL SPROUTS

Ingredients

- 1 (16 oz.) package frozen Brussels sprouts
- 2 apples - peeled, cored, and cut into 3/4-inch chunks
- 2 sweet onions, cut into 3/4-inch chunks
- 2 tbsp extra-virgin olive oil
- salt and ground black pepper to taste
- 1 pinch garlic powder
- zest from 1 lemon
- juice from 1 lemon

Directions

- Set your oven to 425 degrees F before doing anything else.
- In a large bowl, place the frozen Brussels sprouts, apple, onion, olive oil, salt, black pepper and garlic powder and toss to coat.
- Transfer the Brussels sprouts mixture into a large rimmed baking sheet in a single layer.
- Cook in the oven for about 20 minutes.
- Drizzle with the freshly squeezed lemon juice and serve with a sprinkling of the lemon zest.

Amount per serving (6 total)

Timing Information:

Preparation	15 m
Cooking	20 m
Total Time	35 m

Nutritional Information:

Calories	88 kcal
Fat	4.6 g
Carbohydrates	12.1g
Protein	0.8 g
Cholesterol	0 mg
Sodium	29 mg

* Percent Daily Values are based on a 2,000 calorie diet.

I ♥ Brussels Sprouts

Ingredients

- 2 lb. Brussels sprouts, trimmed and halved lengthwise
- 1 C. coarsely chopped pecans
- 2 tbsp olive oil
- 2 cloves garlic, finely chopped
- kosher salt and ground black pepper to taste

Directions

- Set your oven to 400 degrees F before doing anything else.
- In a large bowl, add the Brussels sprouts, pecans, olive oil and garlic and toss to coat well.
- Transfer the Brussels sprouts mixture into a large rimmed baking sheet in a single layer.
- Cook in the oven for about 20-25 minutes.

Amount per serving (8 total)

Timing Information:

Preparation	15 m
Cooking	20 m
Total Time	35 m

Nutritional Information:

Calories	174 kcal
Fat	13.5 g
Carbohydrates	12.3g
Protein	5.1 g
Cholesterol	0 mg
Sodium	79 mg

* Percent Daily Values are based on a 2,000 calorie diet.

LEMON AND DIJON BRUSSELS SPROUTS

Ingredients

- 1 lb. Brussels sprouts
- 2 cloves garlic, thinly sliced
- 1/2 tsp cayenne pepper
- 1/2 tsp crushed red pepper flakes
- 2 green onions, chopped
- 2 tbsp Dijon mustard
- 1 tbsp lemon juice
- salt and ground black pepper to taste

Directions

- Arrange a steamer basket in a pan of the boiling water.
- Place the Brussels sprouts, garlic, cayenne pepper and red pepper flakes in the steamer basket and cook, covered for about 30 minutes.
- Drain well and transfer the Brussels sprouts into a bowl.
- Add the green onions, mustard, lemon juice, salt and pepper and toss to coat.

Amount per serving (4 total)

Timing Information:

Preparation	15 m
Cooking	30 m
Total Time	45 m

Nutritional Information:

Calories	64 kcal
Fat	0.4 g
Carbohydrates	< 13.4g
Protein	4.1 g
Cholesterol	0 mg
Sodium	218 mg

* Percent Daily Values are based on a 2,000 calorie diet.

ONION CLOVES AND BROWN SUGAR BRUSSELS SPROUTS

Ingredients

- 1 1/2 lb. Brussels sprouts
- 3 tbsp butter
- 1 onion, finely chopped
- 1/4 C. all-purpose flour
- 2 C. beef broth
- salt and pepper to taste
- ground cloves to taste (optional)
- 2 tbsp brown sugar
- 2 tbsp lemon juice

Directions

- In a large pan of lightly salted boiling water, cook the Brussels sprouts, covered for about 7-10 minutes.
- Drain well.
- In another large pan, melt the butter and sauté the onion till browned.
- Remove the pan from the heat and stir in the flour till smooth.

- Return the pan on low heat and cook, stirring continuously till the flour is lightly browned.
- Slowly, add the beef broth, stirring continuously.
- Stir in the Brussels sprouts, salt, pepper, cloves, brown sugar and lemon juice and simmer for about 5 minutes.

Amount per serving (8 total)

Timing Information:

Preparation	15 m
Cooking	30 m
Total Time	45 m

Nutritional Information:

Calories	114 kcal
Fat	4.8 g
Carbohydrates	15.8g
Protein	4.2 g
Cholesterol	11 mg
Sodium	324 mg

* Percent Daily Values are based on a 2,000 calorie diet.

GARDEN PARTY BRUSSELS SPROUTS

Ingredients

- 3/4 lb. Brussels sprouts, trimmed
- 1/2 C. butter
- 2 medium cucumbers, cut into 1/2 inch chunks
- 1/4 C. all-purpose flour
- 2 C. milk
- 2 tsp chicken bouillon
- 1/8 tsp pepper

Directions

- Set your oven to 350 degrees F before doing anything else.
- In a large pan of lightly salted boiling water, cook the Brussels sprouts, covered for about 5 minutes.
- Drain well.
- In a skillet, melt the butter on medium heat and cook the cucumbers for about 5 minutes.
- With a slotted spoon, transfer the cucumbers into a bowl and keep aside.
- Add the flour into the butter and stir till a roux forms.
- Add the milk, bouillon and pepper and cook, stirring continuously for about 2 minutes.

- In a baking dish, mix together the Brussels sprouts and cucumbers.
- Place the roux and gently toss to coat well.
- Cook in the oven, covered for about 20 minutes.

Amount per serving (8 total)

Timing Information:

Preparation	20 m
Cooking	35 m
Total Time	55 m

Nutritional Information:

Calories	172 kcal
Fat	12.9 g
Carbohydrates	11.5g
Protein	4.3 g
Cholesterol	35 mg
Sodium	127 mg

* Percent Daily Values are based on a 2,000 calorie diet.

Double Apple and Thyme Brussels Sprouts

Ingredients

- 1 C. diced apple
- 1 lb. Brussels sprouts, trimmed and quartered
- 1/4 C. apple cider
- 4 tsp olive oil
- 2 tsp minced fresh thyme
- 1/2 tsp salt
- 1/4 tsp ground black pepper

Directions

- Set your oven to 375 degrees F before doing anything else.
- In a baking dish, mix together the Brussels sprouts, apple, apple cider, olive oil, thyme, salt and pepper.
- Cook in the oven for about 25 minutes.

Amount per serving (4 total)

Timing Information:

Preparation	10 m
Cooking	25 m
Total Time	35 m

Nutritional Information:

Calories	116 kcal
Fat	5.2 g
Carbohydrates	16.7g
Protein	4 g
Cholesterol	0 mg
Sodium	321 mg

* Percent Daily Values are based on a 2,000 calorie diet.

MARIA'S TURKEY BACON BRUSSELS SPROUTS

Ingredients

- 6 slices turkey bacon, diced
- 1 onion, diced
- 1 tbsp minced garlic
- 1 C. chicken stock
- 2 (16 oz.) packages Brussels sprouts, trimmed and halved lengthwise

Directions

- Heat a deep skillet on medium-high heat and cook the bacon, onion, and garlic for about 10 to 12 minutes.
- Add the chicken stock, Brussels sprouts and bring to a boil while scraping the browned from the bottom of the pan with a wooden spoon.
- Cook, covered for about 15 minutes.

Amount per serving (6 total)

Timing Information:

Preparation	15 m
Cooking	25 m
Total Time	40 m

Nutritional Information:

Calories	212 kcal
Fat	13.2 g
Carbohydrates	17.9g
Protein	9 g
Cholesterol	19 mg
Sodium	387 mg

* Percent Daily Values are based on a 2,000 calorie diet.

ONTARIO BACKROAD BRUSSELS SPROUTS

Ingredients

- 2 tbsp duck fat
- 2 lb. Brussels sprouts, trimmed and halved lengthwise
- salt and freshly ground black pepper to taste
- 1 pinch cayenne pepper
- 1 lemon, juiced

Directions

- Set your oven to 450 degrees F before doing anything else and line a baking sheet with the parchment paper.
- In a small pan, melt the duck fat completely.
- In a large bowl, mix together the Brussels sprouts, salt, black pepper, cayenne pepper and melted duck fat and mix till well combined.
- Transfer the Brussels sprouts into the prepared baking sheet.
- Cook in the oven for about 15-20 minutes, flipping once in the middle way.
- Serve with a drizzling of the freshly squeezed lemon juice.

Amount per serving (4 total)

Timing Information:

Preparation	20 m
Cooking	15 m
Total Time	35 m

Nutritional Information:

Calories	125 kcal
Fat	3.1 g
Carbohydrates	23.4g
Protein	8 g
Cholesterol	2 mg
Sodium	< 106 mg

* Percent Daily Values are based on a 2,000 calorie diet.

MEDITERRANEAN BRUSSELS SPROUTS

Ingredients

- 1/4 C. olive oil
- 3 lbs Brussels sprouts, trimmed, & sliced thin
- 1/2 C. shallot, minced
- 1 tbsp fresh thyme
- 1/2 C. water
- 2 tbsp fresh lemon juice
- salt & pepper

Directions

- In a large nonstick pan, heat the oil on high heat and sauté the Brussels sprouts for about 6-7 minutes.
- Stir in the shallots and thyme and sauté for about 2-3 minutes.
- Stir in the water and cook for about 1 minute.
- Remove from the heat and stir in the lemon juice, salt and pepper.

Servings per Recipe: 8

Timing Information:

Preparation	
Cooking	15 mins
Total Time	23 mins

Nutritional Information:

Calories	129.2
Fat	7.6g
Carbohydrates	0.0mg
Protein	37.6mg
Cholesterol	14.1g
Sodium	4.6g

* Percent Daily Values are based on a 2,000 calorie diet.

FRUIT MEDLEY BRUSSELS SPROUTS

Ingredients

- 1/2 lb. Brussels sprouts
- 1 tbsp olive oil
- 1/4 C. chopped cashews
- 1/4 C. apple juice
- 1/2 C. dried craisins
- 1 tbsp freshly grated ginger

Directions

- In a food processor, add the Brussels sprouts and pulse till shredded.
- In a skillet, heat the olive oil on medium heat and cook the shredded Brussels sprouts for about 5 minutes.
- Reduce the heat to low and stir fry the cashews for about 2 minutes.
- Stir in the apple juice, craisins and ginger and simmer for about 5 minutes.

Amount per serving (4 total)

Timing Information:

Preparation	10 m
Cooking	15 m
Total Time	25 m

Nutritional Information:

Calories	154 kcal
Fat	8.5 g
Carbohydrates	20.3g
Protein	2.7 g
Cholesterol	0 mg
Sodium	15 mg

* Percent Daily Values are based on a 2,000 calorie diet.

EXPERIMENTAL TARRAGON BRUSSELS SPROUTS

Ingredients

- 2 lb. Brussels sprouts, trimmed and halved lengthwise
- 1 C. coarsely chopped brazil nuts
- 2 tbsp olive oil
- 2 cloves garlic, finely chopped
- 1 tsp ground tarragon
- kosher salt and ground black pepper to taste

Directions

- Set your oven to 400 degrees F before doing anything else.
- In a large bowl, add the Brussels sprouts, tarragon, Brazil nuts, olive oil and garlic and toss to coat well.
- Transfer the Brussels sprouts mixture into a large rimmed baking sheet in a single layer.
- Cook in the oven for about 20-25 minutes.

Amount per serving (8 total)

Timing Information:

Preparation	15 m
Cooking	20 m
Total Time	35 m

Nutritional Information:

Calories	174 kcal
Fat	13.5 g
Carbohydrates	12.3g
Protein	5.1 g
Cholesterol	0 mg
Sodium	79 mg

* Percent Daily Values are based on a 2,000 calorie diet.

THANKS FOR READING! JOIN THE CLUB AND KEEP ON COOKING WITH 6 MORE COOKBOOKS....

http://bit.ly/1TdrStv

 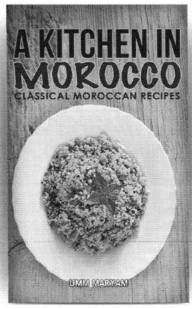 

To grab the box sets simply follow the link mentioned above, or tap one of book covers.

This will take you to a page where you can simply enter your email address and a PDF version of the box sets will be emailed to you.

Hope you are ready for some serious cooking!

http://bit.ly/1TdrStv

COME ON...
LET'S BE FRIENDS :)

We adore our readers and love connecting with them socially.

Like BookSumo on Facebook and let's get social!

Facebook

And also check out the BookSumo Cooking Blog.

Food Lover Blog